Teaching Investigative Skills

Book 4
Ages 10–11

Chris Tooley

The author, Chris Tooley, is an Advanced Skills Teacher (AST) working in Cambridgeshire. He has practical experience of working with teachers across a wide range of schools.

Acknowledgements

I would like to offer my thanks to my wife, Joanna, who has been a significant influence in shaping the materials and unstinting in support and encouragement. Also to Shân Oswald, Senior Science Advisor for Cambridgeshire, and all the primary colleagues who played an important part.

Editor: Rebecca Harman
Layout artist: Suzanne Ward
Cover design: Duncan McTeer
Cover image: Tony Anderson/Getty Images
Illustrations: Jean de Loren

First published 2003 by Folens Limited.
Reprinted 2003.

Every effort has been made to contact copyright holders of material used in this publication. If any copyright holder has been overlooked, we should be pleased to make any necessary arrangements.

British Library Cataloguing in Publication Data. A catalogue record for this publication is available from the British Library.

ISBN 1 84303 017-9

Contents

Introduction

The materials in this book form the fourth part of the foundation skills for scientific enquiry at Key Stage 2 and develop the skills learned in Years 3,4 and 5.

Skills sessions

Lesson plans, OHTs and Pupil Sheets for the following topics:

● Drawing line graphs
● Describing patterns.

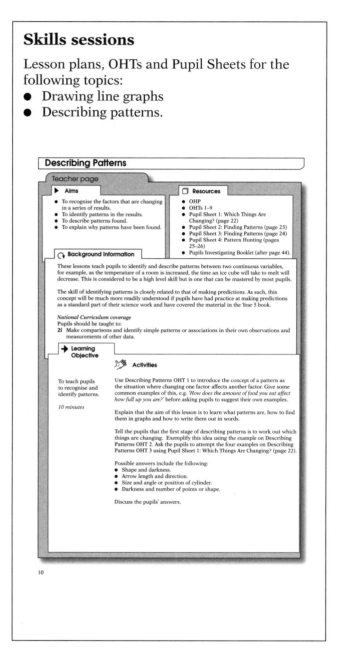

Pupil Sheets

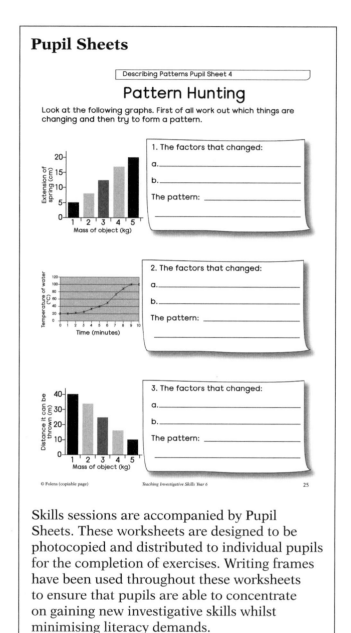

Skills sessions are accompanied by Pupil Sheets. These worksheets are designed to be photocopied and distributed to individual pupils for the completion of exercises. Writing frames have been used throughout these worksheets to ensure that pupils are able to concentrate on gaining new investigative skills whilst minimising literacy demands.

Practical application sessions

Each skills session is followed by lesson plans, linked to QCA units, detailing the reinforcement of the skills in an overtly scientific and practical context.

At the end of each lesson plan there is a list of other investigative activities that can be used to further embed the skills. These examples have been drawn from the Year 6 QCA units.

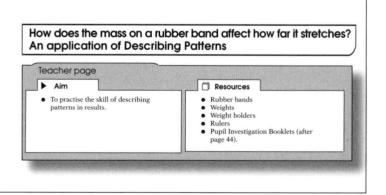

Planning Cards and Planning Sheets

Two discrete resources have been provided to aid the all-important planning process of investigations. Either is suitable for use in the teaching of this skill and all subsequent investigative lessons. However, individual teachers may prefer one or the other format.

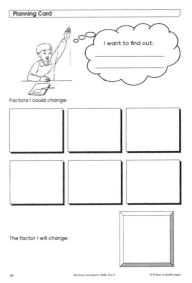

The Planning Card, which can be found on pages 40–41, can be used in conjunction with Post-its to provide pupils with a 'hands on' planning framework for the identification of factors to be investigated. This is best accomplished by photocopying the two pages back to back and then laminating the sheet. This ensures that the cards can be used time after time for any planning activities.

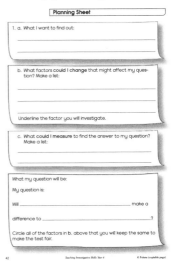

The Planning Sheet, which can be found on pages 42–43, provides a writing frame that pupils can use in two ways. The Planning Sheet can be photocopied and laminated to provide a quick, reusable reference for pupils when writing up an investigation, or the sheet can be photocopied and given to pupils to use as a writing frame, which can then be fixed into their science books.

Pupil Investigation Booklet

The Pupil Investigation Booklet for Year 6 can be found after page 44. To construct the booklet, simply photocopy the four individual sheets back to back and then fold and staple the resulting two sheets.

The booklets can be used in two ways:
- In conjunction with the skills sessions to provide immediate reference to the key learning points and writing frames introduced in the session.
- When carrying out any subsequent practical investigations. The booklets provide a single location where pupils can gain help and reminders when encountering any of the taught skills. Pupils should be encouraged to use this resource rather than immediately asking the teacher as, in this way, pupils can be encouraged to develop a personal working understanding of skills, so becoming increasingly independent in their work.

A copy of the booklet can be given to each pupil so that annotations can be added, or class sets can be made and re-used from year to year.

Whole investigations

Three full investigations have been provided on pages 29–39. These can be used towards the end of Year 6 to practise the whole range of investigative skills and to inform teacher assessment.

Background

Origins and development

The materials in this book were developed in response to numerous requests from primary colleagues and advisory teachers for a coherent scheme to teach the skills of scientific enquiry (Sc1).

The following skills are focused on:

- Forming questions

- Predictions

- Planning fair tests

- Tables

- Graphs

- Conclusions

- Evaluations.

These specific skills were chosen for a number of reasons:

- To lay a sound foundation of skills for primary pupils to interact with the scientific knowledge and understanding required at Key Stage 2.

- To reflect the emphasis on Sc1 in the end of Key Stage National Curriculum assessments.

- To enable pupils to approach investigative work with confidence at Key Stage 2 and beyond.

The initial materials, aimed at Year 6 classes, were trialled in a group of over 35 schools. Responses from teachers were positive and further modifications were made to include Year 5. This scheme was then adopted by Cambridgeshire LEA and recommended to all primary schools.

The success of this scheme led to calls for the development of complementary materials for Years 3 and 4. These were duly completed and tested in classroom trials. The whole programme was then revised to form a complete Key Stage 2 scheme.

Classroom trials of the complete Key Stage 2 schemes led to further positive feedback including an OFSTED report that noted, 'this systematic programme is proving an effective foundation for teaching good lessons very sharply focused on scientific skills.'

The nature of the materials

Early discussions with primary school teachers, backed up by a review of published materials, suggested that normal practice for pupils to learn the skills of scientific enquiry was by the following:

- Meeting the skills for the first time within the context of a practical investigation.

- Being asked to deal with several new skills at the same time.

It was found that a more profitable way to introduce these key skills was for pupils to be taught the skills individually and in a context free from the competing 'noise' of practical work. In this way, the skills themselves would take centre stage as the sole learning objective.

Accordingly, each new skill is introduced in a theoretical session, and outlined in a detailed lesson plan using overhead transparencies to communicate new ideas to pupils. Although non-practical, the design of the session and accompanying worksheets has focused upon ensuring that all pupils are actively involved in the learning process.

The application of the skills in practical contexts is vital if pupils are to gain a full understanding of the scientific process. To this end, follow up activities have been developed (referenced to QCA units) to accompany each skills session.

The final components of the materials are the Pupil Investigation Booklets that accompany each year at Key Stage 2. These booklets can be photocopied and used as a first resort, encouraging pupils to develop increasing independence in investigative work.

This structure is most simply described using the diagram below:

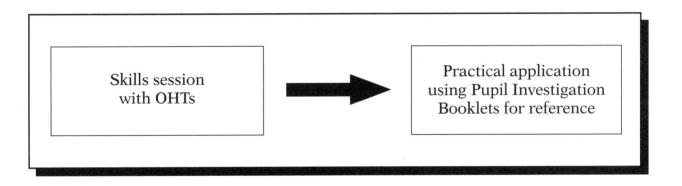

Progression of materials over the key stage

The skills taught in each successive year reinforce and build upon those developed earlier. Years 3 and 4 concentrate on foundation skills, dealing with discontinuous factors (discrete variables), whereas Years 5 and 6 concentrate on the relationships between continuous factors (continuous variables). The culmination of this work comes in Year 6 when pupils are challenged to complete a number of whole investigations. This development can be most clearly appreciated in the table on page viii.

Skill Area	Year 3	Year 4	Year 5	Year 6
Forming Questions	Identifying key factors and introducing the terms, *'The factor I changed'* and *'The factor I measured'*.	Using factors to suggest what will happen in an investigation.	Forming questions for investigation and making predictions.	Using factors to plan fair tests and describing patterns in results.
Predictions	Suggesting the outcomes of a range of circumstances involving discrete factors (variables). Explaining ideas, often using everyday knowledge and understanding.	Making predictions with increasing use of simple scientific facts to explain ideas.	Suggesting the outcomes of a range of circumstances involving continuous factors (variables). Explaining ideas, often using scientific facts.	Making predictions over a range of contexts using scientific facts to justify ideas.
Planning Fair Tests	Identifying the factors to be controlled to make simple, fair tests involving a small number of factors.	With help, planning fair procedures and considering whether tests are fair or not.	Developing clear, step-by-step instructions to fairly investigate questions set by the teacher.	Planning and carrying out fair investigations with increasing independence.
Tables	With help, producing simple tables, mostly involving one series of data.	Increasingly producing simple tables independently (using Pupil Investigation Booklets).	With help, producing tables involving more than one series of data.	Independently producing tables involving more than one series of data (using Pupil Investigation Booklets).
Graphs	With help, producing simple bar graphs.	Producing simple bar graphs with increasing independence (using Pupil Investigation Booklets).	Independently producing simple bar graphs or, with help, line graphs.	With help, producing line graphs.
Conclusions	Saying what was found out in an investigation.	Saying what was found out in an investigation and, increasingly, using simple scientific facts to explain the findings.	Saying what was found out in an investigation and using simple scientific facts to explain the findings.	Identifying and describing patterns found between continuous factors (variables) and using scientific facts to explain these findings.
Evaluations		Looking back at investigative work and suggesting one point that could be improved.	Looking back at investigative work and suggesting two or more points that could be improved.	Considering a whole investigation and suggesting two or more points that could be improved and how it would be done.

Drawing Line Graphs

Teacher page

▶ Aim

● To teach pupils how a series of data can be converted into a line graph.

☐ Resources

● OHP
● OHTs 1–4
● Graph paper
● Pupil Investigation Booklet (after page 44).

↻ Background Information

This session provides a context within which the skill of drawing line graphs can be introduced or refined in a scientific context.

National Curriculum coverage
Pupils should be taught to:
2h Use a wide range of methods, including ... line graphs ... to communicate data in an appropriate and systematic manner.

➡ Learning Objectives

⟍⟍ Activities

To practise the identification of factors in a scientific question.

To revise the organisation of a series of raw data into a table.

15 minutes

Use Drawing Line Graphs OHTs 1 and 2 to present a question for investigation. Read through the question and ask the pupils to identify the following:
● The factor being changed (time saucepan is on cooker).
● The unit of the factor being changed (minutes).
● The factor being measured (temperature of water in saucepan).
● The unit of the factor being measured (°C).

Discuss their answers with the class. Ask them to consider whether the results shown have been recorded in the best way and whether they can suggest improvements that could be made. Discuss the pupils' ideas.

Ask the pupils to use the guidelines in their Pupil Investigation Booklets (after page 44) to construct a table for these results.

As a matter of convention the factor being changed should be written in ascending order, i.e. 0, 1, 2, 3 etc. with the start term being written as 0.

To review attempts at table design.

10 minutes

Ask one pupil to draw their table on the board. Ask the other pupils to note the positive features of the table and then to comment on anything that could be improved. Use Drawing Line Graphs OHT 3 to show an example version of the table.

Drawing Line Graphs

 **Learning
Objectives**

 Activities

To construct a line
graph.

15 minutes

Use Drawing Line Graphs OHT 4 as a prompt to encourage pupils to consider
how tabulated data can be made easier to understand.

Ask the pupils to convert the information into a line graph. The way in which
you choose to approach this will depend largely upon the amount of graph
work that pupils have covered to date. You may like to use this occasion as
an opportunity to teach pupils this skill. Should this be the case, a suitable
method would be:
1. Draw axes
2. Scale axes evenly
3. Label axes
4. Plot points
5. Join points to make a line
6. Add a title.

Where pupils are already familiar with line graphs, they may be able to
attempt the graph independently.

Whichever method is chosen, pupils should use their Pupil Investigation
Booklets to refer to the criteria for good line graphs.

To consider
whether graphs
have been correctly
constructed.

10 minutes

Ask the pupils to swap line graphs. Ask them to use the criteria on
Drawing Line Graphs OHT 5 to mark the line graphs. The pupils can then
make any corrections necessary to score 10 points.

9 minutes – 100°C

2 minutes – 23°C

6 minutes – 50°C

4 minutes – 33°C

10 minutes – 100°C

7 minutes – 72°C

8 minutes – 90°C

3 minutes – 27°C

1 minutes – 21°C

Start – 20°C

5 minutes – 40°C

Put these results into a table.

Your table should look like this:

Time on cooker (minutes)	Temp of water (°C)
0	20
1	21
2	23
3	27
4	33
5	40
6	50
7	72
8	90
9	100
10	100

Graph to show the heating of a saucepan of water

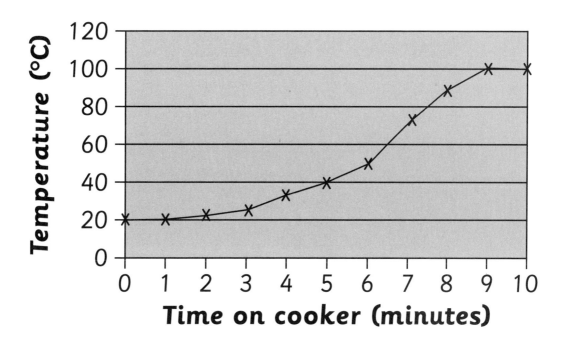

How good was your graph? Mark your own graph using the list below:

Title saying what the graph is showing	1 point
Axes drawn with a pencil and ruler	1 point
Axes labelled temperature and time	2 points
Units used: minutes and °C	2 points
Both axes numbered evenly: 10, 20, 30, 40, etc.	2 points
Points plotted correctly	1 point
Points joined with a pencil	1 point

How many did you score out of 10?

Now make changes to your graph to score 10 points!

What affects the size of shadows?
An application of Drawing Line Graphs

▶ Aim

- To practise the skill of drawing line graphs.

🗍 Resources

- Light source
- Card
- Rulers
- Lollipop sticks
- Glue
- Pupil Investigation Booklet (after page 44)
- Planning Card (pages 40–41) or Planning Sheet (pages 42–43).

↻ Background Information

Shadows are formed when opaque objects stop light passing through them. The size of the shadow is dependent upon the size of the object, and the distance and angle of the light source; **QCA Unit 6f**: How We See Things.

Where QCA units have been followed pupils will have met the concept of how shadows are formed.

→ Learning Objectives

🖑 Activities

To introduce the question to be investigated.

5 minutes

Explain the following context to the class:
The local council have decided to grant permission for the building of a huge tower block in the centre of the town. The block has been specially designed to be attractive to the eye and will be floodlit from its most attractive side so that people will be able to see it from miles around. However, some local residents are complaining that the shadow cast by the block will deprive them of light. The council have hired you, a firm of investigative scientists, to investigate the size of the shadow that will be produced.

Ask the pupils to use a Planning Card (pages 40–41) or Planning Sheet (pages 42–43) to suggest the range of factors that might affect the size of shadow produced.

Possible answers include the following:
- The size of the tower block.
- The distance away of the floodlights.
- The angle the floodlights hit the building.

Discuss the pupils' ideas and choose one factor to investigate. Since the tower block is a certain height, size is not the best factor to investigate. The distance away of the lighting makes a much more suitable factor to choose.

To plan a fair test.

10 minutes

Ask the pupils to work in groups and plan a fair test to investigate the problem. Discuss ideas with the class and agree on a common procedure that can be written on the board.

What affects the size of shadows?
A application of Drawing Line Graphs

Teacher page

 Learning Objectives

 Activities

A suitable procedure might be:
1. Cut out a model of the tower block in card and stick the base on to a lollipop stick.
2. Stand the model 10cm from a wall or screen.
3. Place the light source 10cm from the model and measure the height of the shadow.
4. Move the light source back 10cm at a time, each time measuring the height of the shadow formed.

To carry out a fair test.

10 minutes

Discuss the construction of a results table and produce it on the board. Carry out the investigation as a class with the pupils setting up the equipment and taking measurements.

To construct a line graph of the results.

30 minutes

Ask the pupils to use the prompts in their Pupil Investigation Booklets to construct their own line graph. When they have finished their graphs, ask the pupils to check their work using the criteria in the Pupil Investigation Booklets and then to help other pupils still at work.

To consider the conclusions of the investigation.

5 minutes

Ask the pupils what recommendations they would give to the town council regarding the floodlighting of their new tower block.

Further investigations where this skill could be reinforced

QCA Unit 6a: *Interdependence and Adaptation*
Plan an investigation on which pupil in the class has the strongest finger muscles.

QCA Unit 6c: *More About Dissolving*
Plan an investigation on which type of gas moves through the air quickest.

QCA Unit 6d: *Reversible and Irreversible Changes*
Plan an investigation on the effect of wind on the drying of a wet cloth.

QCA Unit 6e: *Forces in Action*
Plan an investigation on how the direction of a shadow changes during the course of a day.

Describing Patterns

▶ Aims

- To recognise the factors that are changing in a series of results.
- To identify patterns in the results.
- To describe patterns found.
- To explain why patterns have been found.

▢ Resources

- OHP
- OHTs 1–9
- Pupil Sheet 1: Which Things Are Changing? (page 22)
- Pupil Sheet 2: Finding Patterns (page 23)
- Pupil Sheet 3: Finding Patterns (page 24)
- Pupil Sheet 4: Pattern Hunting (pages 25–26)
- Pupils Investigating Booklet (after page 44).

↻ Background Information

These lessons teach pupils to identify and describe patterns between two continuous variables, for example, as the temperature of a room is increased, the time an ice cube will take to melt will decrease. This is considered to be a high level skill but is one that can be mastered by most pupils.

The skill of identifying patterns is closely related to that of making predictions. As such, this concept will be much more readily understood if pupils have had practice at making predictions as a standard part of their science work and have covered the material in the Year 5 book.

National Curriculum coverage
Pupils should be taught to:
2i Make comparisons and identify simple patterns or associations in their own observations and measurements of other data.

➡ Learning Objective

To teach pupils to recognise and identify patterns.

10 minutes

Activities

Use Describing Patterns OHT 1 to introduce the concept of a pattern as the situation where changing one factor affects another factor. Give some common examples of this, e.g. *'How does the amount of food you eat affect how full up you are?'* before asking pupils to suggest their own examples.

Explain that the aim of this lesson is to learn what patterns are, how to find them in graphs and how to write them out in words.

Tell the pupils that the first stage of describing patterns is to work out which things are changing. Exemplify this idea using the example on Describing Patterns OHT 2. Ask the pupils to attempt the four examples on Describing Patterns OHT 3 using Pupil Sheet 1: Which Things Are Changing? (page 22).

Possible answers include the following:
- Shape and darkness.
- Arrow length and direction.
- Size and angle or position of cylinder.
- Darkness and number of points or shape.

Discuss the pupils' answers.

Describing Patterns

 Learning Objectives

 Activities

To teach pupils how to look for patterns in results.

5 minutes

Remind the pupils that a pattern describes how changing one factor affects another. For example, if one factor is getting bigger, what happens to the other factor? Is it getting bigger, smaller or staying the same?

Use the flower and bee example on Describing Patterns OHT 4 to give examples of this process. Ask the pupils to identify the factors being changed before trying to identify a pattern.

Use Describing Patterns OHT 5 to reinforce this process with the class (the bigger the spider, the smaller the web).

To practise the identification of factors that are changing and to look for a pattern.

15 minutes

Give the pupils a set amount of time to complete Pupil Sheet 2: Finding Patterns (page 23), answering the questions on Describing Patterns OHT 6.

Possible answers include the following:
● The larger the circle, the darker the shading.
● The bigger the fire, the higher the temperature.

Discuss pupils' responses. Give the pupils a set amount of time to complete Pupil sheet 3: Finding Patterns (page 24) and answer the questions on Describing Patterns OHT 7. Possible answers include the following:
● The faster the speed, the greater the distance ran.
● The bigger the bell, the further away it could be heard.
● The larger the apple, the heavier it is.
● No pattern.

Explain that sometimes there will be no pattern but this does not mean the investigation has failed. No pattern can be just as valid a finding as a clear pattern.

When discussing the pupils' answers, note down all of the descriptive words used, for example:
● Faster
● Heavier
● Darker
● Hotter.

To apply the skills of finding patterns using real scientific data in the form of graphs.

10 minutes

Use Describing Patterns OHT 8 to show how the skills of describing patterns can be related to graphs. Remind the pupils of the fact, introduced in Drawing Line Graphs, that the reason for drawing a graph is to clearly show any patterns in results.

Ask the pupils to examine the graph and identify the factor being changed and the factor being measured. Make the point that this is a very easy task when considering a graph, as the factors being changed and measured are always the same as the labels on the axes.

An effective memory technique (as described in the Year 4 book) for remembering which axis shows the factor being changed is for pupils to hold out their arms horizontally and to change the shape of their hands (the factor being changed). They can then pretend that they are pulling down a tape measure vertically (the factor being measured).

Describing Patterns

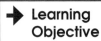

→ Learning Objective

 Activities

Ask the pupils to try to describe the pattern shown on the graph. Pupils normally suggest answers such as: *'The longer the saucepan was on the cooker, the hotter it got'*. Stress that this type of answer is correct, but that there is an easier and more consistent way to describe a pattern without having to use words like hotter, faster, longer, heavier, etc.

Use Describing Patterns OHT 9 in conjunction with page 6 of the Pupil Investigation Booklet to show how the pattern of words can be used as a standard way of describing patterns.

To practise the identification of patterns in graphs.

Ask the pupils to complete the first graph exercise on Pupil Sheet 4: Pattern Hunting (pages 25–26). Discuss the answer with the pupils before asking them to complete the remainder of the sheet.

20 minutes

Discuss all of the exercises.

Which two things are changing in the example below?

The two things changing are:
a. the size of the triangle
b. the darkness of the triangle.

Which two things are changing in each of these examples?

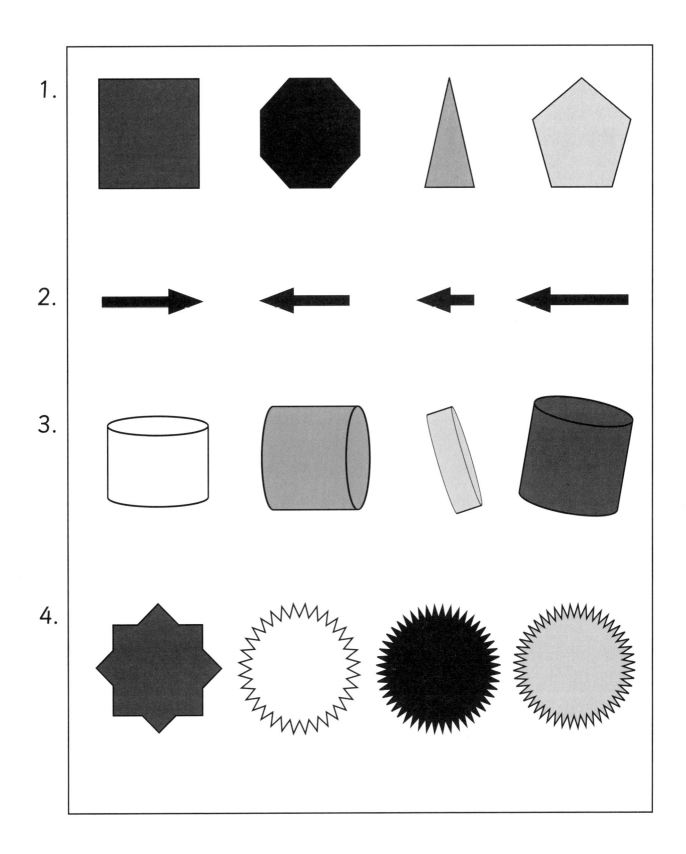

1.

2.

3.

4.

Describing Patterns OHT 3

What two things are changing in this picture?

The size of the flower and the number of bees.

Can you find a pattern?

What is happening to the number of bees as the size of the flower gets bigger?

As the size of the flower gets bigger, the number of bees gets larger.

Now try this one:

For each example write down the two factors that are changing and then try to write down the pattern that links them.

1.

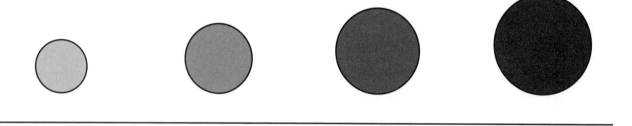

2.

Temperature   300°C   180°C   220°C   120°C

Now try these:

3. Speed 6kph   10kph   3kph   8kph

How far he   12km   20km   6km   16km
ran in 2
hours

4.

Distance away
that the sound
could be heard

80m   60m   20m   100m

5.

Mass   100g   200g   300g   425g   600g   1000g

6.

Graph to show the heating of a saucepan of water

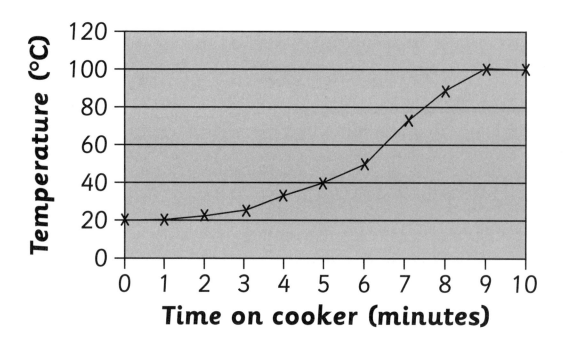

The factor that you changed always goes on the x-axis (horizontal): Time of heating.

The factor that you measured always goes on the y-axis (vertical): Temperature of water.

To describe a pattern use this phrase:

My graph shows that when

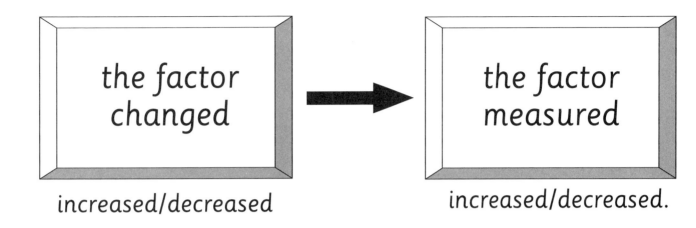

the factor changed → the factor measured

increased/decreased increased/decreased.

First put in the names of the things that are changing:

My graph shows that when

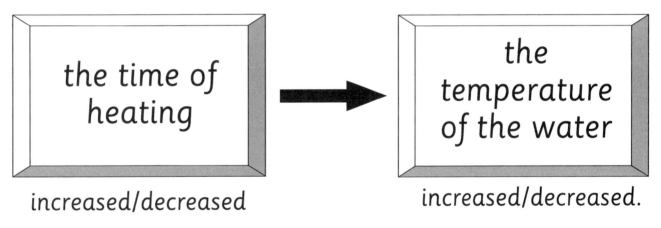

the time of heating → the temperature of the water

increased/decreased increased/decreased.

Then choose the correct words from the options:

My graph shows that when

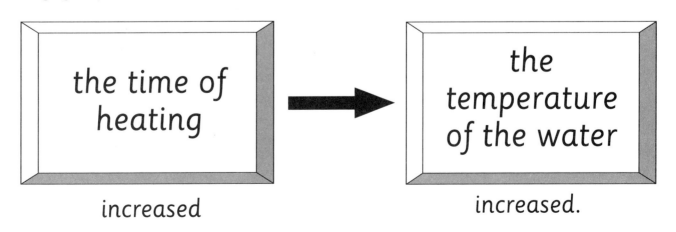

the time of heating → the temperature of the water

increased increased.

Which Things Are Changing?

1. Which things are changing?

   a. _____

   b. _____

2. Which things are changing?

   a. _____

   b. _____

3. Which things are changing?

   a. _____

   b. _____

4. Which things are changing?

   a. _____

   b. _____

Teaching Investigative Skills Year 6

Finding Patterns

1. Which things changed?

    a. _____

    b. _____

As the _____ gets _____

the _____ gets _____

2. Which things changed?

    a. _____

    b. _____

As the _____ gets _____

the _____ gets _____

Finding Patterns

3. Which things changed?

    a. _____

    b. _____

As the _____ gets _____

the _____ gets _____

4. Which things changed?

    a. _____

    b. _____

As the _____ gets _____

the _____ gets _____

5. Which things changed?

    a. _____

    b. _____

As the _____ gets _____

the _____ gets _____

6. Which things changed?

    a. _____

    b. _____

As the _____ gets _____

the _____ gets _____

Teaching Investigative Skills Year 6

Pattern Hunting

Look at the following graphs. First of all work out which things are changing and then try to form a pattern.

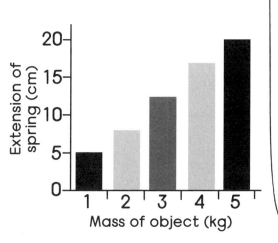

1. The factors that changed:

a._____

b._____

The pattern: _____

_____

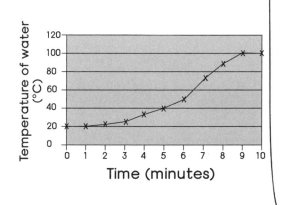

2. The factors that changed:

a._____

b._____

The pattern: _____

_____

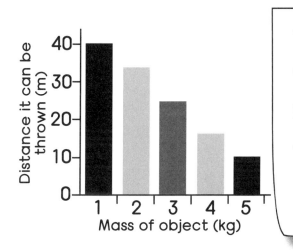

3. The factors that changed:

a._____

b._____

The pattern: _____

_____

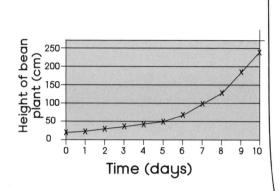

4. The factors that changed:

a._____

b._____

The pattern: _____

_____

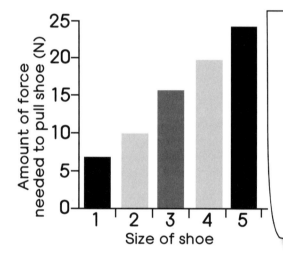

5. The factors that changed:

a._____

b._____

The pattern: _____

_____

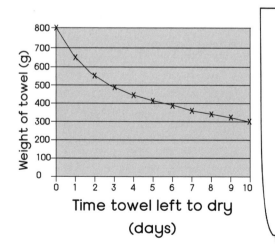

6. The factors that changed:

a._____

b._____

The pattern: _____

_____

Teaching Investigative Skills Year 6

How does the mass on a rubber band affect how far it stretches?
An application of Describing Patterns

▶ Aim

- To practise the skill of describing patterns in results.

☐ Resources

- Rubber bands
- Weights
- Weight holders
- Rulers
- Pupil Investigation Booklets (after page 44).

↻ Background Information

The amount by which a rubber band stretches is directly proportional to the weight hung from it. For example, if the mass is doubled, the extension of the rubber band also doubles. However, this relationship does not go on indefinitely. Once the elastic limit of a material is reached the material changes in its properties and, in the case of the rubber band, expands quickly and breaks; **QCA Unit 6e**: Forces in Action.

Where QCA units have been followed pupils will have been introduced to the meaning of the term force.

➡ Learning Objectives

Activities

Learning Objectives	Activities
To introduce the question to be investigated and obtain results. *10 minutes*	Ask the pupils to describe what they understand by the term 'elastic'. Discuss their answers and ask for suggestions of elastic materials. Explain that the aim of this lesson is to investigate elastic materials. Ask the pupils to suggest what factors might affect the amount that a rubber band stretches. Possible answers include the following: ● Thickness of rubber band. ● Colour of rubber band. ● Length of rubber band. ● Amount of mass hung from rubber band. Discuss the pupils' answers before investigating the effect of mass on the amount a rubber band stretches.
To plan a fair test. *10 minutes*	With the class watching, deliberately carry out the test in an unfair manner. For example, measure the rubber band from different places, use different rubber bands; hang weights on different places, etc. Ask the pupils to comment on whether the test was fair or not and which alterations would make the test fair.
To carry out a fair test. *20 minutes*	Ask the pupils to carry out the fair test in groups. They should record their results in a simple table constructed with reference to their Pupil Investigation Booklets. **SAFETY** ● Warn pupils regarding the safe handling of rubber bands. Excessive weight will cause the bands to snap and whip back. Tell the pupils the maximum mass to be used. ● Ensure that rubber bands are suspended from a firm object. In the absence of stands, placing the band around a pencil over a gap between adjacent tables will be adequate.

How does the mass on a rubber band affect how far it stretches?
An application of Describing Patterns

 Learning Objectives

 Activities

To plot the results on a line graph.	Ask the pupils to enter their results in a table prepared on the board. Calculate the average of each series of data. Ask the pupils to suggest how the results could be presented in a more understandable form.
10 minutes	Ask the pupils to explain how to draw a line graph. Carry out the instructions on the board. This graph does not need to be accurate; it is the shape that should be clear.
To describe a pattern in the results.	Challenge the pupils to use their Pupil Investigation Booklets to describe the pattern shown in the line graph and to write this out.
30 minutes	

Further investigations where this skill could be reinforced

QCA Unit 6b: *Micro-organisms*
What affects the rate at which bread goes mouldy?

QCA Unit 6c: *More About Dissolving*
What affects the rate of dissolving?

QCA Unit 6e: *Forces in Action*
What affects the speed at which spinners fall?

QCA Unit 6f: *How We See Things*
What affects the size of a shadow?

QCA Unit 6g: *Changing Circuits*
What affects the brightness of a bulb connected to a circuit?

What affects the rate at which a spinner falls?
Whole Investigation

Teacher page

▶ Aim

- To carry out a whole investigation.

🗇 Resources

- Spinner templates (pages 32–34)
- Paper clips
- Stopwatches
- Pupil Investigation Booklet (after page 44)
- Planning Card (pages 40–41) or Planning Sheet (pages 42–43)
- 2m lengths of string.

↻ Background Information

Air resistance is a force that acts to resist any object moving through air. The amount of air resistance depends on a combination of the surface area of the object moving through the air and the degree to which it is aerodynamic; **QCA Unit 6e**: Forces in Action.

Spinners provide an effective context within which ideas of air resistance can be investigated and clear results gained. The aim of this investigation is to examine the effect of wing size on the rate of falling. Templates of three different sizes of spinners are provided for photocopying.

Pupils often suggest that the spinners must be the same mass if the test is to be fair. This can be approximately achieved by attaching one standard sized paper clip to the biggest spinner, two to the middle sized spinner and three to the smallest spinner.

Session 1

➡ Learning Objectives

Activities

To revise the meaning of the term air resistance and to set the context for the investigation.

10 minutes

Hold up a spinner in one hand and a scrunched up piece of paper in the other. Ask the pupils to predict the difference in the rate of falling to the ground. Discuss the concept of air resistance.

To form a scientific question to investigate.

10 minutes

Ask the pupils the question, *'What affects the time a spinner takes to drop 2m?'* and ask them to use a Planning Card (pages 40–41) or Planning Sheet (pages 42–43) to identify the factors that might affect this.

Possible answers include the following:
- The mass of the spinner.
- The size of the wings.
- The material the spinner is made from.
- The way in which the spinner is dropped.

Select the factor, the size of the spinner's wings, to investigate.

Ask the pupils which factor they could measure to find out how long the spinner takes to fall (time taken to fall 2m).

Ask the pupils to note down the full question to be investigated. For example, *'My question is: Will the size of the spinner's wing make a difference to the time taken for it to fall 2m?'*

What affects the rate at which a spinner falls?
Whole Investigation

 Learning Objectives

 Activities

To make
a justified
prediction.

15 minutes

Ask the pupils to use their Pupil Investigation Booklets (after page 44) to form a justified prediction for this investigation.

A good prediction might be: *'As the size of the spinner increases, the time taken for it to fall 2m also increases. I think that this will happen because I know that the larger the wings, the more air resistance there will be to slow the spinner down'.*

Discuss the pupils' predictions and reasons giving no indication of which are correct.

To plan a fair test.
To write a series of
clear instructions.

10 minutes

Show the pupils the three different sized spinners that will be used in the investigation. Through class discussion, produce a list of the factors that will need to be kept the same to ensure a fair test.

Ask the pupils to work in small groups to produce a series of instructions that could be followed to complete the fair test. Any pupils finishing early can start to design a results table.

Discuss the different plans produced and build up an agreed procedure for the investigation. Ensure that this includes repeating the investigation at least two additional times. Ask the pupils to write down their own series of instructions. A good way of ensuring the height dropped remains constant is to use some lengths of string pre-cut to 2m.

To construct three
spinners for the
investigation.

To test the action of
the spinners.

15 minutes

Use the template for large spinners (page 34) to demonstrate how to make a spinner from the templates provided. Ask the pupils to make spinners. Once made, give the pupils a few minutes to try out their plan and see if their spinners will spin!

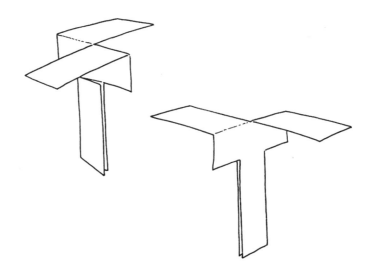

What affects the rate at which a spinner falls?
Whole Investigation

Session 2

 Learning Objectives

 Activities

Learning Objectives	Activities
To reinforce the nature of the investigation.	Talk through the procedure that the pupils are to carry out and clarify the time limits for achieving the set activity.
To produce a results table.	Stagger the beginning of the practical by asking the pupils to use their Pupil Investigation Booklets (after page 44) to construct a results table, including a column for averages, before collecting their spinners.
15 minutes	
To carry out a fair test in which measurements are accurately recorded.	Give clear time limits for the completion of the practical aspect of the investigation and the calculation of averages.
30 minutes	
To describe patterns found in the results.	Write one set of results into a table on the board. Sketch a simple graph of the data. Ask the pupils to use their Pupil Investigation Booklets to describe the pattern shown in the results.
To explain any pattern found using scientific knowledge.	Ask the pupils to identify why the larger spinners fell most slowly. Encourage them to use their scientific ideas about air resistance.
15 minutes	

Spinners!

Spinners!

Spinners!

Spinners!

Spinners!

Spinners!

Spinners!

Spinners!

Teaching Investigative Skills Year 6

Spinners!

Spinners!

Spinners!

Spinners!

Teaching Investigative Skills Year 6

fold

Spinners!

fold

fold

Spinners!

fold

fold

fold

fold

fold

Teaching Investigative Skills Year 6

What affects the brightness of a bulb?
Whole Investigation

Teacher page

▶ Aim

- To carry out a whole investigation.

↻ Background Information

▯ Resources

- Batteries
- Connecting wires
- Fuse wires of varying thickness and material
- Bulbs
- Planning Card (pages 40–41) or Planning Sheet (pages 42–43)
- Pupil Investigation Booklets (after page 44).

This investigation looks at the effect of changing the thickness of fuse wire on the brightness of a bulb in a circuit; **QCA Unit 6g**: Changing Circuits.

The brightness of a bulb increases as the amount of electrical current flowing through it increases. This can be achieved by increasing the voltage of the batteries supplying the circuit (or their number) or by decreasing the overall resistance of the circuit. Fuse wire has a higher resistance than normal conducting wire and comes in a variety of values, for example, 1 amp, 2 amp, 3 amp and 5 amp. The higher the value of the wire, the lower its resistance to the flow of electrical current.

As the fuse wire gets thicker the bulb shines brighter as more electrical current is able to travel through the bulb, in the same way as a wider road allows a greater volume of cars to travel down it. As the wire gets longer, the bulb shines less brightly. This is because the overall resistance of the wire to electrical current increases. Each different type of wire has a different resistance.

Session 1

→ Learning Objective

To form a question for investigation by identifying the factors involved.

15 minutes

✍ Activities

Ask the pupils to draw a circuit diagram of a simple circuit containing a bulb, battery, switch and connecting wires. Ask one pupil to draw this on the board, then ask for a volunteer to build the circuit.

Show the pupils the brightness of the bulb when the switch is pressed. Explain that someone has suggested that putting a very thin wire into this circuit will alter the brightness of the bulb. Demonstrate this by putting a length of thin fuse wire into the circuit. The bulb will dim.

Ask the pupils to suggest some reasons why the bulb dimmed.

Ask the pupils to use a Planning Card (pages 40–41) or Planning Sheet (pages 42–43) to identify the factors that might affect the question, *'How does the wire affect the brightness of the bulb?'* Choose the factor to be investigated. If possible have groups investigating each of the possible variables.

Possible answers include the following:
- Length of the wire.
- Material the wire is made from.
- Thickness of the wire (which can be varied by twisting wires together).

Ask the pupils to suggest ways in which they could measure the brightness of the bulbs. The factor to be measured is difficult to judge, as it cannot be measured directly (unless a datalogger with light probe is available).

What affects the brightness of a bulb?
Whole Investigation

 Learning Objectives

 Activities

However, pupils can make judgements of whether the bulb was brighter or dimmer than for the previous test.

Ask the pupils to use their Pupil Investigation Booklets (after page 44) to form a question for investigation.

To form justified predictions that can be tested.

15 minutes

Ask the pupils to use their Pupil Investigation Booklets to make predictions for the particular factor being investigated.

Discuss the pupils' ideas. Give no indication of whether their ideas are correct or not.

To turn ideas into a form that can be investigated and decide how to carry out a fair test.

10 minutes

Discuss why it is important to ensure that tests are fair. Ask the pupils to make a list of the factors needed to be controlled to make the test fair.

To produce a series of written instructions to investigate the question.

20 minutes

Ask the pupils to write a series of instructions detailing how to investigate the problem. Ask them to read out their instructions to another member of the class who judges whether they are clear enough.

Session 2

 Learning Objective

 Activities

To carry out safely an investigative procedure.

30 minutes

Ask the pupils to carry out their tests and use their Pupil Investigation Booklets to record their results in an appropriate form. One pupil from each group should be chosen to put the results of their investigation on the board.

What affects the brightness of a bulb?
Whole Investigation

 Learning Objectives

 **Activities**

To identify and describe patterns in the results.

To try to explain any patterns in the results.

10 minutes

Ask the pupils to use their Pupil Investigation Booklets to note down any patterns in the results and to discuss why these results were gained. Warn pupils in advance that they may be asked to explain their results to the class.

To discuss patterns in the results and suggest explanations.

10 minutes

Ask each group to explain any patterns found in their results and to give explanations about why these results were gained. Discuss the explanations as a class.

To evaluate an investigation.

10 minutes

Ask the pupils to use the criteria given in their Pupil Investigation Booklets to write an evaluation of their plans.

What affects the rate of dissolving?
Whole Investigation

Teacher page

▶ Aim

- To carry out a whole investigation.

▭ Resources

- Sugar types; granulated, brown, icing and caster sugar
- Spatulas
- Weighing machine to measure amounts of sugar
- Stirrers
- Beakers
- Timers
- Measuring cylinders
- Planning Card (pages 40–41) or Planning Sheet (pages 42–43)
- Pupil Investigation Booklet (after page 44).

↻ Background Information

The rate at which sugar dissolves is dependent on a number of factors (**QCA Unit 6c**: More About Dissolving):

The amount of water: As the amount of water increases, the speed of dissolving increases as there are more water molecules for the sugar particles to fit between.

The temperature of the water: As the temperature of the water increases, the speed of dissolving increases as the molecules of water are moving faster when it gets hotter.

The amount of sugar: As the amount of sugar increases, the speed of dissolving decreases as there is more sugar to be dissolved in the same amount of water.

The size of the sugar particles: As the size of the sugar particles increases, the speed of dissolving decreases as water can get to the sugar easier when the particles are smaller.

The amount of stirring: As the amount of stirring increases, the speed of dissolving increases as the water mixes quicker with the sugar particles.

The type of sugar: Some sugars are more soluble than others.

Session 1

→ Learning Objective

To form a question for investigation by identifying the factors involved.

15 minutes

Activities

Ask the pupils to consider the question, *'Does sugar always dissolve at the same speed?'* Ask them to use a Planning Card (pages 40–41) or Planning Sheet (pages 42–43) to identify the range of factors that might affect this.

Possible answers include the following:
- Amount of water.
- Temperature of water.
- Amount of sugar.
- Size of sugar particles.
- Amount of stirring.

Discuss the pupils' answers and choose a factor for investigation.

Ask the pupils to suggest ways in which they could measure how quickly sugar dissolves. All of their suggestions should involve time in some context.

Ask the pupils to note down a finalised question for investigation, for example, *'I want to find out how the amount of the water affects the time taken for sugar to dissolve.'*

What affects the rate of dissolving?
Whole Investigation

 Learning Objectives

 Activities

To form justified predictions that can be tested. *15 minutes*	Ask the pupils to use their Pupil Investigation Booklets to discuss their question in groups and to make predictions. Discuss the pupils' predictions and explanations as a class.
To turn ideas into a form that can be investigated and decide how to carry out a fair test. *30 minutes*	Show the pupils the range of equipment available for the investigation. Ask them to list the factors that should be controlled if their test is to be fair. Ask the pupils to work in groups to produce their own list of instructions to investigate the question they have developed. Ask the pupils to check each other's plans and to decide whether they are clear and fair. Select pupils to read out their plans with other pupils following the instructions to the letter using the available equipment. Discuss how clear the plans were.

Session 2

 Learning Objectives

 Activities

To carry out a fair test. *40 minutes*	Ask the pupils to collect their equipment and carry out their investigation, noting down their results in rough. If time is available, the investigation should be repeated.
To present a set of data in the form of a table of results. *20 minutes*	Ask the pupils to use their Pupil Investigation Booklets to present their data in the form of a table with headings and units.
To present a set of data in the form of a line graph. *40 minutes*	Discuss with the pupils which group's results are suitable for putting on a line graph (e.g. volume of water, temperature, number of stirs, amount of sugar) and which can only be shown on a bar graph (e.g. particle size, type of sugar). Ask the pupils to use their Pupil Investigation Booklets to produce a line graph or bar graph of their results.
To identify patterns in a graph. *20 minutes*	Ask the pupils to consider the graphs produced in their investigation and to identify the factor being changed and the factor being measured. Ask them to use this information and their Pupil Investigation Booklets to describe the patterns shown.

Planning Card

I want to find out:

_____

_____

Factors I could change:

The factor I will change:

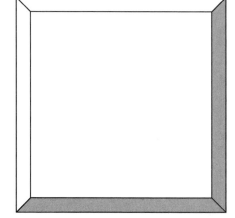

Planning Card

What I am going to change

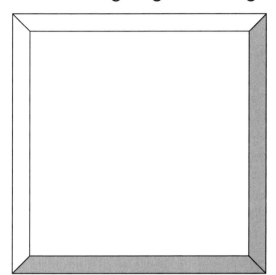

What I am going to measure

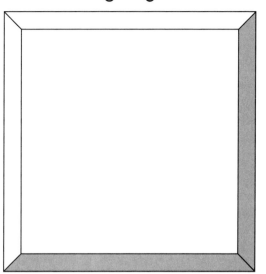

My question is will...

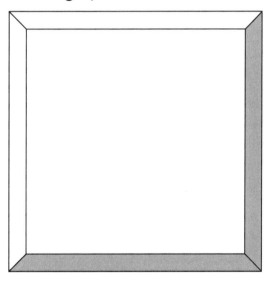

make a difference to...

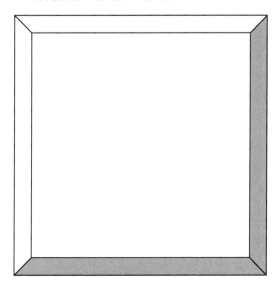

Planning Sheet

1. a. What I want to find out:

_____

_____

b. What factors **could I change** that might affect my
   question? Make a list:

_____

_____

_____

Underline the factor you will investigate.

c. What **could I measure** to find the answer to my question?
   Make a list:

_____

_____

What my question will be:

My question is:

Will _____ make a

difference to _____?

Circle all of the factors in **b.** above that you will keep the same to
make the test fair.

Teaching Investigative Skills Year 6

HOW TO CREATE ...
Your Guide to Science Investigations Booklet

STEP 1

Photocopy the title page.

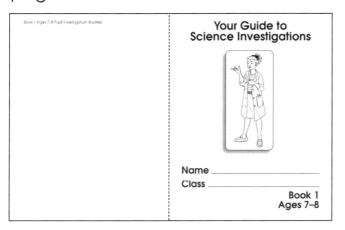

STEP 2

On the back of the title page photocopy pages 2 and 7.

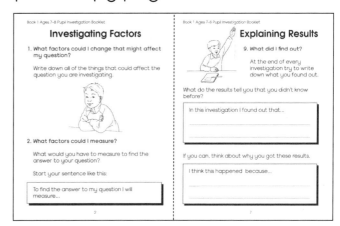

STEP 3

Photocopy pages 6 and 3.

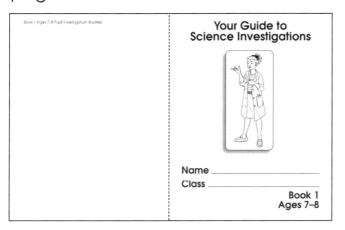

STEP 4

On the back of pages 6 and 3 photocopy pages 4 and 5.

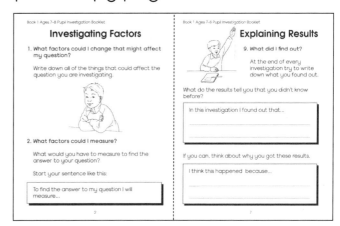

STEP 5

Put the copied sheets together to make the booklet.

Staple if necessary.

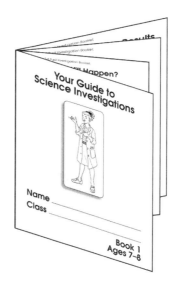

Your Guide to Science Investigations

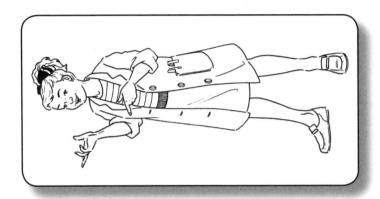

Book 4
Ages 10–11

Name

Class

Forming Questions

1. What factors could I change that might affect my question?

Write down all of the things that could affect the question you are investigating.

2. What factors could I measure?

What would you have to measure to find the answer to your question?

Start your sentence like this:

To find the answer to my question I will measure…

3. What will my question be?

| My question is will the | factor I change | make a difference to the | factor I measure? |

Evaluations

12. How good was my investigation?

a. Was the question being investigated clear?

b. Was the test fair?

c. Were the results noted down clearly?

d. Is there anything wrong with the conclusion?

e. Is there anything else that is missing in this report?

f. What would you change to make the test better?

Predictions

4. What I think will happen.

What will happen to what you are measuring when you change the factor you are investigating?

Use the example below to help you:

I think that when the

factor I change

is (increased, decreased)   the

factor I measure

will (increase, decrease).

5. Why I think this will happen.

Explain why you think that your prediction is correct. Start your explanation like this:

I think that this will happen because I know that

_____

_____

_____

Describing Patterns

10. The pattern I found.

Note down the things you can see that are changing.
Now try to see if you can describe the way these things are changing in a pattern.

Use the example below to help you.

My results show that
when the

factor I change

is (increased, decreased)   the

factor I measure

will (increase, decrease).

11.   Was my prediction correct?

Look back at your prediction. Was it right or wrong?

Try to explain why you got this answer.

This is the same as/different from my prediction. I think this happened because...

Planning

6. What I will do.

Make a numbered list of instructions saying exactly how you will carry out the investigation.

7. Making the test fair.

Make a list of the things that you will keep the same to make the test fair.

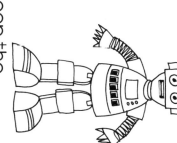

8. Presenting results.

Whenever you collect results write them down.

Often the easiest way to note them down is in a table with headings and units.

Try to follow the pattern shown below:

What I changed	What I measured (units)

Drawing Graphs

9. Drawing graphs.

When you draw a bar graph or a line graph remember to:

- Choose a scale just bigger than your largest numbers.
- Space numbers out evenly.
- Label both axes – the vertical axis with units.
- Give your graph a title.
- Use a sharp pencil.

What I measured (unit) e.g. Temperature (⁰C)

What I changed (unit) e.g. Time (minutes)

Folens

Teaching Investigative Skills in Science

BOOK 1 AGES 7–8

TEACHING INVESTIGATIVE SKILLS

Develop pupils' intellectual skills for carrying out practical investigations.

Four books for teachers of 7 to 11 year olds, containing:

- Lesson plans
- Photocopiable OHTs
- Photocopiable pupil sheets

NEW!

Provides teachers with practical investigations by which pupils can apply their intellectual skills, plus extensive lists of ideas for further applications.

The series provides teachers with a collection of non-practical lessons to promote an understanding of:

- the nature of prediction
- the concept of variables
- different types of variables
- collecting and presenting data
- fair testing
- planning
- evaluating results.

All activities are referenced to the QCA Units and help to prepare pupils for Sc1 dimension of the revised KS2 SAT

Drawing Line Graphs

teacher page

Aims
- To teach pupils how a series of data can be converted into a line graph.

Learning Objective

This session provides a context within which the skill of drawing line graphs can be introduced or refined in a scientific context.

Background Information

National Curriculum coverage
Pupils should be taught to:
2h Use a wide range of methods, including ... line graphs ... to communicate data in an appropriate and systematic manner.

Activities

Resources
- OHP
- OHTs 3–4
- Graph Paper
- Pupil Investigation Booklets (after page 38)

Making Predictions

What Will Happen? Pupil Sheet 1

1. What do you predict will happen when a piece of chocolate is left lying in the hot summer sun?

... hot a piece of chocolate left lying in the hot summer sun

... predict will happen when a raw egg is cracked into a hot ...

... the water will

... raw egg cracked into a hot frying pan will

Teaching Investigative Skills, Year 3

19

TEACHING INVESTIGATIVE SKILLS IN SCIENCE
Each book is £14.95

FC0144	Book 1	(Age 7–8)
FC0152	Book 2	(Age 8–9)
FC0160	Book 3	(Age 9–10)
FC0179	Book 4	(Age 10–11)

Folens Publishers, Apex Business Centre, Boscombe Road, Dunstable, Beds LU5 4RL Phone: 0870 609 1237 Fax: 0870 609 12...

▼ PHOTOCOPY & FAX OR POST ▼

PRIMARY SCIENCE RESOURCES

Please send me on 28 days' evaluation:

TEACHING INVESTIGATIVE SKILLS IN SCIENCE

- ☐ FC0144 Book 1 (Age 7–8)
- ☐ FC0152 Book 2 (Age 8–9)
- ☐ FC0160 Book 3 (Age 9–10)
- ☐ FC0179 Book 4 (Age 10–11)

PHOTOPACKS – £14.95 each

- ☐ F5232 Our Bodies
- ☐ F5224 Minibeasts

PRIMARY SUPPORT – Book + CD Pack

- ☐ BA2042 Life Processes and Living Things
- ☐ BA2069 Materials and Their Properties
- ☐ BA2050 Physical Processes

IDEAS BANK

- ☐ FA4901 Investigating Life Processes
- ☐ FA605X Investigating Materials
- ☐ FA6068 Investigating Physical Processes

Name: _____

School: _____

Address: _____

_____

Postcode: (Vital) ☐☐☐☐☐☐☐

Tel: _____

Fax: _____

Email: _____

Signature: _____

Special offers are only available to UK schools ordering direct from Folens. Price, product, publication details are correct at the time of going to press, but are subject to change with... VAT is payable on all non-book products and is shown where applicable. Evaluation is o... to UK schools. UK P&P £3.95 per order.

☎ 0870 609 1235   📠 0870 609 1236   orders@folens.com   www.folens.c...